HOW TO SPY ON A
SHARK

Lori Haskins Houran

Illustrated by
Francisca Marquez

Albert Whitman & Company
Chicago, Illinois

Take a boat ride
out to sea
until you spy a fin.

Get all set
to get all wet
and *splash!*
go diving in.

Glide beside
a mako shark.

Spot a mako pup.

Call out to the crew
to grab a net
and scoop it up!

Grip the pup
and flip it over.

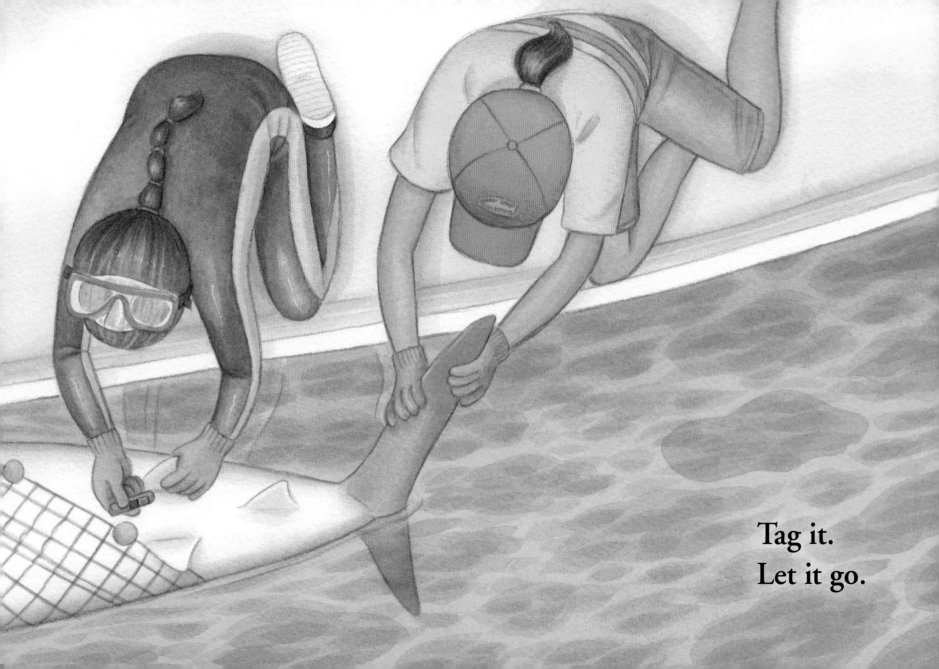

Tag it.
Let it go.

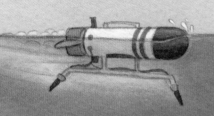

Drop a *robot* in the sea
to follow it below!

The mako twists!
The robot turns!
They dart and dip and dive.

The robot shoots a video
and sends it to you live!

Track the pup
for miles and miles.

Find out where it eats,

how far and fast
and deep it swims,

and who the mako meets!

Spy until it's time to go.
Soon it will be dark.

Lift the robot
from the sea…

So long, little shark!

Why spy on a shark?

Sharks have been around for more than 400 million years—since *before* the dinosaurs! But many species are in danger of going extinct. Marine biologists spy on sharks so they can help them. How far do sharks travel? Do they like cold or warm water, deep or shallow? Where do their pups grow up? The more scientists find out, the better they can protect sharks and their habitats.

Glide beside a mako shark

One way to spy on a shark? Dive in and swim along! It's a challenge to keep up with sharks, though—especially makos, who can move 35 miles an hour. Swimming with sharks is risky too. Sharks don't hunt humans, but if a person gets in their way, they just might take a bite. Still, shark attacks are pretty rare. Around the world, more people are killed by jellyfish than sharks!

Grip the pup and flip it over

Sometimes marine biologists put tags on sharks so they can keep track of them. The tags make sounds that the scientists pick up with underwater microphones. (The sharks can't hear the sounds at all.) How do you tag a shark without getting bitten? Flip it over. When a shark is upside down, it goes into a *tonic* state. In other words, it falls asleep! Once the shark is turned right side up again, it's back in action.

So long, little shark!

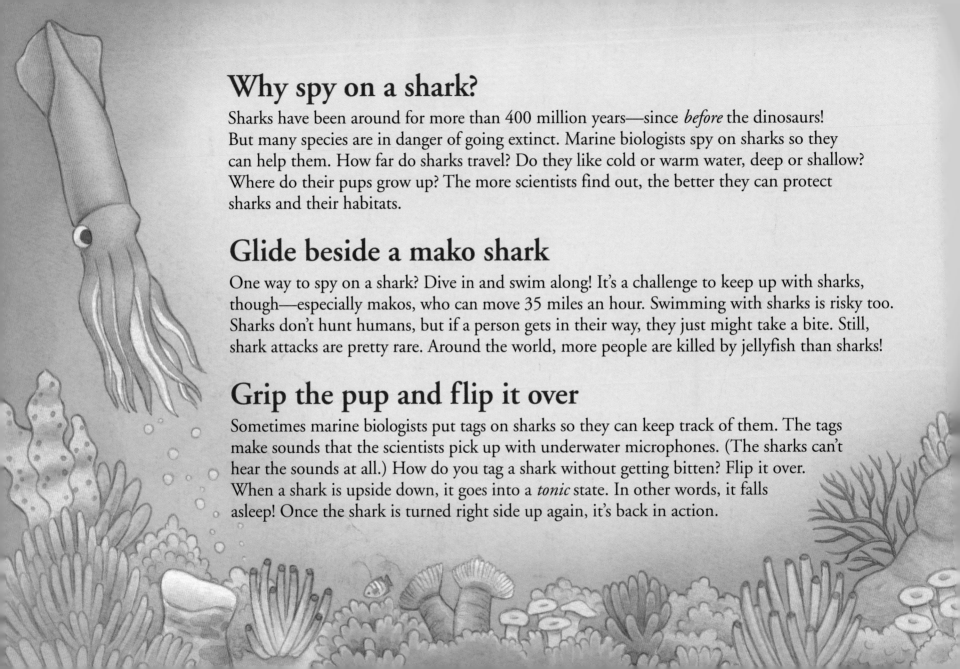

Why spy on a shark?

Sharks have been around for more than 400 million years—since *before* the dinosaurs!
But many species are in danger of going extinct. Marine biologists spy on sharks so they
can help them. How far do sharks travel? Do they like cold or warm water, deep or shallow?
Where do their pups grow up? The more scientists find out, the better they can protect
sharks and their habitats.

Glide beside a mako shark

One way to spy on a shark? Dive in and swim along! It's a challenge to keep up with sharks,
though—especially makos, who can move 35 miles an hour. Swimming with sharks is risky too.
Sharks don't hunt humans, but if a person gets in their way, they just might take a bite. Still,
shark attacks are pretty rare. Around the world, more people are killed by jellyfish than sharks!

Grip the pup and flip it over

Sometimes marine biologists put tags on sharks so they can keep track of them. The tags
make sounds that the scientists pick up with underwater microphones. (The sharks can't
hear the sounds at all.) How do you tag a shark without getting bitten? Flip it over.
When a shark is upside down, it goes into a *tonic* state. In other words, it falls
asleep! Once the shark is turned right side up again, it's back in action.

Drop a robot in the sea

Shark spies have a new tool—underwater robots! Each robot is programmed to follow the tag on a shark. Along the way, the robot gathers information: How fast the shark swims. How deep it goes. The temperature of the water around it. The robot even records a video of the shark and the creatures it meets. Back at the lab, the scientists create a 3-D computer animation of the shark's world!

Spy until it's time to go

Marine biologists spend all day spying on a single shark. At the end of the day, they make sure to scoop up their robot. The robots cost about $180,000 apiece! Often the scientists are so excited to study what they've found that they head straight to the lab…and work all night too!

For Nicholas, who loves sharks—LH

For my nephew, Aidan—FM

A thousand thanks to Dr. Christopher G. Lowe of California State University Long Beach Shark Lab (a real-life shark spy!) for his expert help with this book.

Library of Congress Cataloging-in-Publication Data
Houran, Lori Haskins, author.
How to spy on a shark / by Lori Haskins Houran ;
illustrated by Francisca Marquez.
pages cm
Summary: "A crew of scientists at sea use a camera-equipped robotic device to track a shark's movements through the water."—Provided by publisher.
Audience: Ages 4–7.
Audience: K to grade 3.
1. Mako sharks—Juvenile literature. 2. Remote submersibles—Juvenile literature. 3. Marine sciences—Research—Juvenile literature. 4. Marine scientists—Juvenile literature. I. Marquez, Francisca, illustrator. II. Title.
QL638.95.L3H68 2015
597.3'3—dc23   2014023611

Printed in China.
10 9 8 7 6 5 4 3 2 1 HH 18 17 16 15 14

The design is by Jordan Kost.

For more information about Albert Whitman & Company,
visit our web site at www.albertwhitman.com.